A TASTE OF
THE CARIBBEAN

Yvonne McKenley

Thomson Learning
New York

Titles in this series

A TASTE OF

Britain	Italy
The Caribbean	Japan
China	Mexico
France	Spain
India	West Africa

Cover *The Blue Lagoon, on the north coast of Jamaica.*

Title page *A rainbow over the tropical forest of St. Lucia, with the Petit Piton in the background.*

First published in the
United States in 1995 by
Thomson Learning
115 Fifth Avenue
New York, NY 10003

First published in Great Britain in 1994 by
Wayland (Publishers) Ltd.

Library of Congress Cataloging-in-Publication Data
McKenley, Yvonne.
A taste of the Caribbean / Yvonne McKenley.
p.   cm.—(Food around the world)
Includes bibliographical references and index.
ISBN 1-56847-187-4
1. Cookery, Caribbean—Juvenile literature.
2. Food habits—Caribbean Area—Juvenile literature.
3. Caribbean Area—Social life and customs—Juvenile literature.
[1. Cookery, Caribbean. 2. Food habits—Caribbean Area.
3. Caribbean Area—Social life and customs.] I. Title. II. Series.
TX716.A1M34   1995
394.1'2'09729—dc20   94-30603

Printed in Italy

Contents

The Caribbean

The islands

The Caribbean is the name given to the islands in the Caribbean Sea. They are also known as the West Indies. The Caribbean Sea stretches over 1,860 miles from the tip of Florida to the top of South America, where the sea meets the Atlantic Ocean.

The thousands of islands that make up the Caribbean are divided into three

English Harbor, Antigua, is a favorite port of call for sailors from all over the world.

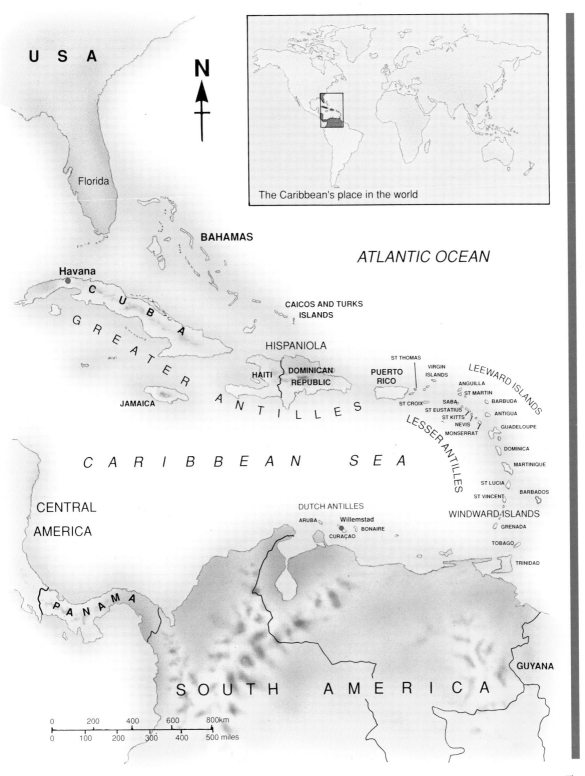

USA

N

Florida

The Caribbean's place in the world

BAHAMAS

ATLANTIC OCEAN

Havana

C U B A

CAICOS AND TURKS
ISLANDS

G R E A T E R   A N T I L L E S

HISPANIOLA

ST THOMAS

VIRGIN
ISLANDS

LEEWARD ISLANDS

HAITI

**DOMINICAN
REPUBLIC**

**PUERTO
RICO**

ANGUILLA

ST MARTIN

JAMAICA

ST CROIX

SABA

ST EUSTATIUS

ST KITTS

NEVIS

MONSERRAT

BARBUDA

ANTIGUA

GUADELOUPE

LESSER ANTILLES

C A R I B B E A N   S E A

DOMINICA

MARTINIQUE

ST LUCIA

ST VINCENT

BARBADOS

CENTRAL

AMERICA

DUTCH ANTILLES

WINDWARD ISLANDS

ARUBA

Willemstad

BONAIRE

GRENADA

CURAÇAO

TOBAGO

P A N A M A

TRINIDAD

GUYANA

S O U T H   A M E R I C A

| 0 | 200 | 400 | 600 | 800km |

| 0 | 100 | 200 | 300 | 400 | 500 miles |

Right *Ugly River in Jamaica. Jamaica, like most Caribbean islands, has high mountains covered with tropical plants.*

Below *Many of the Caribbean islands were formed when volcanoes erupted millions of years ago. Here you can see the black volcanic rocks on the coast of Dominica.*

main groups: the Bahamas, the Greater Antilles, and the Lesser Antilles. Cuba, Jamaica, Hispaniola, and Puerto Rico, the four biggest Caribbean islands, belong to the Greater Antilles. Hispaniola is divided into two countries—Haiti and the Dominican Republic. These four islands of the Greater Antilles make up over 90 percent of the land area of the Caribbean and are home to about 80 percent of the people living there. The Lesser Antilles, a string of smaller islands that lie to the east, are divided into the southern Windward Islands— which include Dominica, Martinique, St. Lucia, Barbados, and Trinidad and Tobago—and the northern Leeward Islands—which include Guadeloupe, Antigua, St. Kitts, and Montserrat. The Bahamas are a group of islands off the southeastern coast of Florida.

Climate

The Caribbean islands lie within the tropics, so the climate is hot all year long. The temperature averages 86°F in the height of summer and rarely goes below 77°F. The Caribbean has a rainy season each year between September and November. Autumn is the hurricane season. Hurricanes are violent storms with winds that can gust up to more than 100 mph and cause tremendous damage and loss of life. Hurricane Gilbert, in 1988, was the worst to hit the Caribbean in more than a hundred years. Many people died, and much of the agriculture in the region was destroyed.

The warm climate, beautiful beaches, and clear seas have made the Caribbean a favorite place for tourists. Tourism has become an important industry for many of the Caribbean countries.

The Caribbean Sea becomes very rough and dangerous during hurricane season.

Many people's idea of a perfect vacation is enjoying the beautiful sandy beaches and clear blue waters of the Caribbean.

A taste of the Caribbean

Right *Mount Pelée, on the island of Martinique, is an active volcano.*

Below *Aruba, which is part of the Dutch Antilles off the coast of South America, is so dry that cactus plants grow all over the island.*

Geography

The geography of the Caribbean islands varies greatly. Some islands, including Barbados and Antigua, are very flat. But most of the islands are mountainous, and some of the mountains were once volcanic. On the French island of Martinique, the volcano Mount Pelée is still active. Mount Pelée last erupted in 1902 killing thousands of people; but it has been quiet ever since.

Some islands have lush rain forests; others are almost as dry as a desert.

History

The Caribbean is named after the warlike Caribs, one of the first peoples to live in the region, mainly on the eastern Caribbean islands. Today, the few Caribs that remain live in communities on the island of Dominica and in Guyana. Also living in the region were the Arawaks, a peaceful people who lived mostly in the western Caribbean islands of Cuba and Jamaica. Both the Caribs and Arawaks had come to the Caribbean from South America.

In 1492, the explorer Christopher Columbus set out from Europe to look for a westward route to Asia across the Atlantic Ocean. At that time, no one in Europe knew that the Americas or the Caribbean existed. When Columbus first came upon the islands of the Caribbean, he thought he had arrived at the Indies in Asia, so he called the people living there Indians.

This picture shows native people welcoming Columbus to the Caribbean and presenting him with gifts. In the background, Columbus's crew is putting up a cross, a symbol of the Christian religion.

Later, when it was realized that these islands were not part of Asia, they were renamed the West Indies.

Columbus claimed the West Indies for Spain. When he returned to Spain, he brought back many strange and wonderful things he had discovered in this "new world" to present to Queen Isabella. These included gold jewelry worn by the Indians, tobacco, strange local food such as sweet potatoes, and native people captured from the islands.

BARCELONA

This picture shows Christopher Columbus presenting Queen Isabella of Spain with jewelry, new foods, and natives that he brought back from the Caribbean.

Columbus returned several times to the Caribbean to claim more islands for Spain and to search for the gold used by the Indians to make their jewelry. He also wanted to find more tobacco because it was becoming very popular in Spain. Spanish settlers soon followed to start farming in what had become known as the New World. They forced the natives to become their slaves and work on the land. The Spanish treated their slaves very cruelly and most of them died from overwork or from diseases brought by the Europeans. Soon there were hardly any native people left in the Caribbean.

By the seventeenth century, other European countries, such as the Netherlands, England, and France, began to invade the area and set up their own colonies. These European countries often fought fierce battles with one another to keep or gain control of the islands.

Above *This Carib woman lives on the island of Dominica.*

Below *These old cannons on the island of Tobago are reminders of the battles that were fought among countries for colonies in the Caribbean.*

Slavery

People were brought to the Caribbean from Africa to work as slaves on the sugarcane plantations. Cutting sugarcane by hand is very hard work, and the cane leaves are razor sharp.

The European settlers grew rich by growing and exporting tobacco to Europe. However, when farmers in Virginia began to export tobacco at cheaper prices, many Caribbean farmers were forced to switch to a new crop—sugarcane.

Sugarcane had been introduced into the Caribbean in the seventeenth century. When it began to replace tobacco as the main export crop, farmers banded together to form large sugarcane plantations. But with so few native people left, the plantation owners needed more workers. This was the beginning of the slave trade in the Caribbean. During the seventeenth and eighteenth centuries, millions of Africans, mainly from West Africa, were shipped to the Caribbean to work as slaves on the plantations. They were chained together and crammed onto slave ships. The journey to the Caribbean took two to three months, and it is estimated that one in three people died on the way.

The British outlawed the slave trade in 1807 and set all slaves free in their Caribbean colonies in 1838. But the slave trade in West Africa was not abolished until the U.S. outlawed slavery in 1865.

When many of the freed slaves left the plantations to run their own farms, plantation owners began to hire indentured laborers from countries such as China and India. These people agreed to work on the plantations for a set period of time for low wages in exchange for their passage. Many indentured laborers stayed in the Caribbean after they had finished their term of work, and their descendants add to the interesting mixture of races and cultures in the Caribbean today.

Above *In some parts of the Caribbean, sugarcane is still cut by hand.*
Below *These indentured laborers from China came to work on the sugarcane plantations.*

The people today

More than 36 million people live in the Caribbean. The population is mainly made up of people whose ancestors came from Africa, Asia, South America, and Europe. Very few pure Caribs remain.

Although there are many large and exciting cities throughout the Caribbean, most people live in small villages in the countryside and work on the land. Trinidad and Tobago are exceptions because they produce oil. Many people on those islands have left the farms and villages to work in the oil industry. The

More than two million people live in Havana, Cuba. Like most large Caribbean cities, Havana was built on the coast and is a busy trading port.

standard of living in Trinidad and Tobago is higher than in any of the other Caribbean countries.

Throughout the Caribbean, religion is an important part of life. Christianity is the major religion. The French and Spanish brought Roman Catholicism to the region; the English brought Anglicanism. But there are many other religions as well.

Many Muslims and Hindus came to the Caribbean from Asia as indentured laborers. Today, over 40 percent of the population of Trinidad are descended from people who came from India and other parts of Asia. In Guyana, they make up over half the total population.

The people living in this hillside village on the island of St. Vincent grow food in the small fields that surround the village.

A taste of the Caribbean

Above *Followers of the Rastafarian religion often have long dreadlocks.*

A new religion called Rastafarianism is becoming very popular among people of African descent. Rastafarians wear their hair in distinctive long braids called dreadlocks. Like Muslims, Rastafarians do not eat pork, and many are vegetarians or vegans.

Most of the countries of the Caribbean have now gained their independence and are no longer colonies. However, they have kept the languages and many of the customs of the countries that colonized them. Today, the people of the Caribbean speak many different languages—Spanish, Dutch, French, and English. In some areas, they also speak Creole, which is a mixture of European and African languages.

With such a diversity of races, religions, and languages, it is no wonder that the Caribbean is a colorful and exciting place. Its interesting mixture of different cultures, traditions, and customs is seen in the enormous choice of avaiable foods.

Store signs in Willemstad, on the Dutch-speaking island of Curaçao, are written in Dutch, Spanish, and English.

Food production

Farming

Because of its warm climate and fertile soils, the Caribbean is an excellent place for agriculture. Before the arrival of the Spanish, the Arawaks and Caribs had

Farmers take their food to town to sell at the open-air markets, like this one in Grenada.

17

A taste of the Caribbean

Right *This man is climbing a coconut palm to pick coconuts. Coconut palms grow in almost all tropical areas. Coconut is a popular ingredient in many Caribbean dishes.*

Below *This sugarcane field in St. Kitts stretches as far as the eye can see.*

cultivated tobacco, cassava, sweet potato, and allspice, which grow naturally in the area. European settlers and traders introduced many new foods such as bananas, mangoes, yams, coconuts, oranges, avocados, limes, and nutmeg, which all grow successfully in the warm Caribbean climate.

The early European settlers grew crops to export back to Europe. Their main export crop was sugarcane, and it remains an important crop even today, especially in Jamaica and Cuba. The sweet juice of the sugarcane is used to make sugar and a sticky brown syrup called molasses. Molasses, in turn, is

Most sugarcane is harvested by machine. It is then taken to factories where it is crushed to make molasses and sugar. Most of the sugar is exported to other countries.

used to make rum. The cane fiber is used to make hardboard, animal feed, and fuel.

Today, bananas have replaced sugarcane as the major export crop in the Caribbean. St. Lucia, in the Windward Islands, has one of the largest banana crops. Grenada, known as the "Spice Isle," exports huge quantities of nutmeg and mace; these spices account for 40 percent of the island's exports. Coffee is produced on a large scale in the mountainous islands. Most of it comes from the Dominican Republic.

This picture shows a nutmeg still inside its fruit. The red, weblike coating on the nutmeg is the spice mace. The mace is removed from the nutmeg and fades to a deep orange.

A taste of the Caribbean

Above *Rice fields in the Dominican Republic.*

Below *Fishing boats and nets on the island of St. Lucia.*

Although the Caribbean has an excellent climate for agriculture, much of the area is too mountainous to grow crops. None of the Caribbean countries grows enough food to feed its own population, so many foods, such as flour and breakfast cereals, are imported.

Fishing

With the great variety of fish available in the Caribbean Sea, fishing has developed into an important, but not a thriving, industry. Cuba is one of the few islands where there is a large-scale fishing industry that provides enough fish and seafood for its own people as well as for export. For the rest of the Caribbean islands, fishing is a small-scale, local activity.

Fruits and vegetables

The hot tropical weather ensures that fresh fruits and vegetables are available all year long to provide a healthy diet.

Root vegetables such as yams and sweet potatoes form an important part of the Caribbean diet. Yams were brought to the Caribbean from Africa. They have dark brown skin and firm yellow or white flesh that is baked or boiled. Sweet potatoes, which are native to the area, are a favorite Caribbean vegetable; they also became very popular with the Spanish. Sweet potatoes come in many varieties, with pink, yellow, red, or orange skins.

Taros are small, hairy-skinned root vegetables that originally came from India. They are closely related to yams and used in much the same way. Taros have a firm white flesh; when cooked they lose their whiteness and turn slightly gray or purple.

Yautias, known as "cocoyams" in Jamaica and "tannia" in Barbados and St. Kitts, are also root vegetables. They are similar in taste and texture to taros

Yams were brought to the Caribbean from Africa. They have become an important part of the Caribbean diet.

and have a leafy stalk known as callaloo. Callaloo (or *calalú*), which is very much like spinach, is a popular vegetable throughout the Caribbean and is often used to make soup.

Chayote, also called christophene, cho-cho, or mirliton, is a pear-shaped fruit with green skin and soft flesh. It is a member of the gourd family and tastes similar to zucchini. Chayotes are usually cooked in soup with vegetables or they are pickled. They were first grown in Mexico.

Breadfruit is a popular Caribbean fruit that grows on large trees and comes from the South Pacific. There are many different kinds of breadfruits, but they are all round with bumpy light-green skins and cream-colored flesh. Breadfruit is cooked like a vegetable; it can be fried, boiled, or roasted. In Jamaica, a favorite way of cooking breadfruit is to roast it, in its skin, over an open fire.

A breadfruit tree. Baked breadfruit has the same texture as bread. It takes the place of rice or potatoes in some Caribbean meals.

Akee, a fruit originally grown in West Africa, is a main ingredient in the Jamaican national dish, akee and salt fish. An akee has a straw-colored to purplish-red skin, or pod, which bursts open when the fruit is ripe. (Unripe or overripe akees are poisonous!) Inside each akee pod there are usually three

Above left *Red akee fruits growing on a tree.*

Above right *An opened akee fruit.*

Below *Bananas can spoil very quickly and easily, so they must be cut while they are still green and unripe.*

bright yellow akees, each with a large black seed attached to it. The seeds and the pod are thrown away, and the soft fruit can be eaten raw or cooked. Cooked akees look and taste a little like scrambled eggs.

Avocados, sometimes called alligator pears, are widely available throughout the Caribbean and are eaten any time of the day. They have dark green skins and a rich-tasting, creamy-textured flesh.

Bananas were introduced to the Caribbean from the South Pacific and are now one of the most important export crops. Bananas grow on "hands," or clusters, which hang from a long flower stalk from the banana tree. An unripe banana is green and gradually turns yellow as it ripens. Bananas are sometimes roasted in their skins, but they are usually eaten raw.

Plantains are a type of large banana

and are always cooked. Fried plantains are eaten with breakfast, lunch, or dinner. Plantains can also be boiled. Unripe plantains are sliced and deep-fried to make plantain chips.

Mangoes were brought to the Caribbean from India and have become a favorite fruit. The skin of a ripe mango usually has a combination of colors, including yellow, red, and green. The sweet flesh is a dark golden color. There is a large seed at the center of the fruit. Unripe mangoes can be used to make mango chutney.

These boys from the Dominican Republic are enjoying fresh mangoes.

Mangosteens are a round, purplish fruit, about three inches in diameter. Mangosteens were grown originally in the Malay region of the East Indies. The mangosteen contains five to seven seeds in a juicy white or yellowish pulp that has a somewhat tart flavor. Although it has a similar name, the mangosteen is not related to the mango.

24

Left *The orange flesh of the papaya has a slightly peppery taste.*

Papayas, also known as pawpaws, are native to the Caribbean. They are large pear-shaped fruits that turn yellowish when ripe. They have orange-yellow flesh with a large cluster of soft black seeds in the center.

Soursop, a fruit that comes from South America, has a green prickly skin and a creamy-white flesh with black seeds in the middle. Its flesh can be used to make cool refreshing drinks or even ice cream.

Above *Soursop fruit is used mainly to make drinks and ice cream.*

Guava trees are native to the Caribbean and South America. The guava fruit is small and round; the flesh inside is dotted with many small seeds that can be eaten. Guava jelly or jam is delicious.

Right *A guava fruit. Guavas can be eaten raw or cooked.*

Caribbean dishes

The barbecue was invented by Carib Indians.

Caribbean cooking is a fragrant and colorful mixture of foods influenced by people who came to the area from West Africa, Europe, India, and China. However, the native Carib people gave the world a great idea for cooking when they invented the barbecue. The Caribs cooked their meat and fish, coated in a special pepper sauce, over a large charcoal grill. Jerk pork and jerk chicken (see the recipe on page 36) are two Jamaican specialities that are cooked over an open grill in much the same way that the Caribs barbecued their food.

The African influence in Caribbean cooking can be seen in the dishes such as *fufu* (dumplings made with cassavas, yams, or plantains) and *bammie,* an African cassava bread.

Settlers from India introduced many curried dishes to the Caribbean. This woman is serving curried lamb.

The Asians brought with them curry and other spices that added new tastes to Caribbean cooking. In Jamaica, curried goat is a favorite dish. In Trinidad, roti, an Indian flat bread, and curried vegetables, fish, and meat dishes are particularly popular.

On the islands of Guadeloupe, Martinique, and Haiti, which were once French colonies, the regional specialties include many chicken and fish dishes, such as *fricassée de poulet au coco* (chicken in coconut milk).

Escovitch, a marinated fish dish, is a Spanish recipe that has become part of Caribbean cooking. *Arroz con camerones,* a shrimp and rice dish that

A taste of the Caribbean

uses Spanish ingredients such as olive oil, is another Caribbean favorite.

In many English-speaking islands, such as Jamaica, patties are popular. These are small, flat pies filled with spicy beef, chicken, or salt fish.

Drinks

A favorite drink of the region is fresh lemonade made from a mixture of lemon or lime juice, sugar, and cold water. This drink can quench the biggest thirst and is quick and easy to make. Fruit punch, made with any combination of tropical fruits, is also a popular drink (see the recipe on page 44).

A traditional Christmas drink is made from sorrel, a type of flower that belongs to the hibiscus family (see the recipe on page 42).

Rum is probably the most famous alcoholic drink from the Caribbean. There are many different types of rum and many rum-based drinks.

These men are pushing an ices cart. Fruit syrups, in the bottles, are poured over cups of packed crushed ice to make refreshing fruit drinks.

28

Celebrations

Caribbean celebrations usually include a mixture of lively music and good food. Typical celebrations are Independence Day (when slaves were freed from captivity), weddings, and birthdays. There are also celebrations on certain Christian, Muslim, and Hindu holy days. For example, *Eid-el-Fitr* is a Muslim

These girls are dressed in white for their First Communion, a Roman Catholic ceremony. Many celebrations are connected with religious events.

A taste of the Caribbean

Children enjoy taking part in Carnival celebrations.

celebration held at the end of Ramadan, the month of prayer and fasting. The Hindu festival of *Diwali*, also known as the Festival of Light, commemorates the triumph of good over evil.

Most islands hold some form of Christmas celebration. St. Kitts is famous for its Christmas and New Year festivities. At Christmas, a favorite dessert is Christmas cake made with dried fruits such as sultanas, raisins, and currants. It is similar to raisin-spice cake, except that the fruits in the

Caribbean Christmas cake are soaked in rum.

The most famous of all Caribbean celebrations is Carnival, held on most islands once a year. Carnival was originally a Roman Catholic festival held just before Lent, which is the 40-day period leading up to Easter. People were expected to give up meat for Lent, so the day before Lent they celebrated with a huge feast. This celebration became known as Carnival, which in Latin means "farewell to meat." Today, Carnival is no longer an especially religious celebration, but a time to sing and dance and have fun. People parade through the streets in brightly colored fancy costumes, usually in the form of birds or animals, and dance to music played by steel bands.

Steel bands were invented by the Trinidadians. The steel pans they play

Steel bands are a part of most Caribbean festivals. The steel drums are made from metal oil barrels and garbage cans. The larger the steel drum, the lower the notes it produces.

A taste of the Caribbean

Dancing, singing, and fancy costumes are part of the Junkanoo Festival, which is celebrated near Christmastime in Jamaica and the Bahamas. Junkanoo is thought to have been a god in the religion of the Arawak Indians.

are made from the tops of empty oil drums or metal garbage cans that have been beaten into segments. Each segment produces a different sound.

The most spectacular Caribbean Carnival is held in Trinidad and Tobago. The largest Carnival in the United States is Mardi Gras (the day before Lent), held in New Orleans. The festivities last for a week and millions of people attend.

At all Carnivals, whether inside or outside the Caribbean, there is a wide variety of food such as roast corn, roti, rice and peas, curried goat, plantains, patties, and many more favorite Caribbean dishes.

Banana bread

Bananas are always picked while they are still green and hard and unripe. A banana that is allowed to turn yellow on the tree loses its flavor.

Ingredients

Serves 8

3½ tblsp. soft butter or margarine
¾ cup brown sugar
4 large ripe bananas
1 large egg
1 cup sifted flour
1 tsp. cinnamon
1 tsp. nutmeg
½ tsp. vanilla extract
1 tsp. baking powder
½ tsp. baking soda
butter or margarine to grease the loaf pan

Equipment

2 bowls
ovenproof dish
mixing spoon
fork
whisk
9 x 5 inch loaf pan
waxed paper
scissors
pot holders

A taste of the Caribbean

1   Preheat the oven to 350°F. Place an ovenproof dish of water at the bottom of the oven.

Be careful when using a hot oven. Ask an adult to help you.

2   Mix the sugar and butter together in a large bowl until they form a creamy texture.

3   Peel the bananas and mash them to a pulp with a fork. Add them to the sugar and butter mixture.

4   In a separate bowl, whisk a large egg. Then add to the sugar, butter, and banana mixture. Stir until it is creamy.

5 Gradually mix in all the cinnamon, nutmeg, vanilla extract, baking powder, baking soda, and flour. Mix together well.

7 Spoon the mixture into the pan and put it on the middle shelf of the oven. Bake for about 50 minutes to 1 hour at 350°F.

6 Cut the waxed paper to the size of the loaf pan. Line the bottom of the pan with the paper and put it in the oven for 3 minutes to warm. Remove the pan with pot holders and butter the sides.

8 When the banana bread is firm but still slightly springy to the touch, remove it from the oven. Let it cool for 10 minutes before turning it out of the pan. This banana bread is best eaten cold.

35

Jerk chicken

Equipment

saucepan
spoon
casserole dish
food processor

Jerk chicken, as well as jerk beef and jerk pork, are traditional Jamaican dishes. The meat is flavored with a thick spicy sauce and then barbecued. There are "jerk stalls," like the one shown here, throughout Jamaica.

Ingredients

Serves 4

¾ oz. allspice berries
1 tsp. chili powder
1 tsp. paprika
3 scallions
salt and pepper
4 chicken pieces

1 Heat the allspice berries in a saucepan over medium heat for 2 or 3 minutes, stirring all the time.

2 Put all the ingredients, except the chicken, into a blender and mix them into a thick paste.

3 Rub the paste onto the chicken pieces and put them in a dish in a refrigerator to marinate for at least 2 hours. The chicken can be left in the refrigerator overnight.

4 Slowly grill or barbecue the chicken pieces for 20 to 30 minutes on each side.

Always be careful when cooking on a grill or barbecue. Ask an adult to help you.

Rice and peas

Ingredients
Serves 4

16 oz. brown quick-
    cooking rice
2½ cups cold water
15 oz. can of red
    kidney beans
    (including the
    liquid)
1½ oz. creamed coconut
half a small onion,
    chopped fine
a sprig of fresh thyme
salt and pepper to
    taste
1 tblsp. margarine

Equipment

large bowl
large saucepan with
    a lid
knife
chopping board
mixing spoon

In the Caribbean, beans are called peas. The "peas" used in this recipe are kidney beans. This woman is cooking rice and peas over an open fire.

1 Rinse the rice with cold water in a large bowl and leave it to one side.

3 Place the creamed coconut in the water along with the chopped onions, thyme, salt, pepper, and margarine. Mix well.

2 Pour the cold water into a large saucepan and put it on the stove over high heat for 15 minutes. Turn the heat off, remove the saucepan, and add the can of kidney beans. The water will turn red.

4 Add the rice to the saucepan and stir. Return the saucepan to the stove and put on the lid. Simmer on very low heat for 25 to 30 minutes. Do not stir. If the rice is too watery, take the lid off the saucepan and simmer for another 10 minutes or until ready.

Always be careful when using a knife and heating up water. Ask an adult to help you.

Baked plantain

Ingredients

Serves 2

1 large ripe
   plantain
2 tblsp. butter or
   margarine

Equipment

large sheet of
   tinfoil
butter knife

Plantains are a type of banana. They are used as a vegetable and must be cooked before eating. Young plantains grow hanging down from a flower stalk in tiny bunches, or "hands." As they grow, the hands slowly turn upward.

1 Peel the plantain.

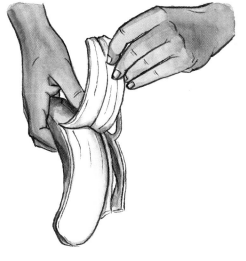

3 Wrap the plantain tightly in the foil.

2 Spread a thin film of butter or margarine over the tinfoil.

4 Bake in the oven at 375°F for 20 minutes. Serve as a side dish.

Be careful when using a hot oven. Ask an adult to help you.

Sorrel

You can get dried sorrel flowers from Asian, African, or Caribbean food stores.

Ingredients
Serves 5

9 oz. dried sorrel
$\frac{1}{2}$ oz. grated ginger
dried orange peel,
    from about half
    an orange
1 whole clove

1 quart water
$\frac{2}{3}$ cup white sugar

Equipment

large bowl
mixing spoon
teakettle
sieve

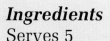

1   Place the sorrel in the bowl, and add the ginger, orange peel, and clove.

2   Boil the water in the teakettle and pour it over the sorrel.

3   Add the sugar and mix. Let the mixture sit out overnight. You may add more sugar to taste if you wish.

4   Strain the mixture through the sieve and serve it with plenty of ice.

Spiced fruit punch

Ingredients
Serves 8
1¼ cup pineapple
  juice
½ cup orange juice
½ cup lemon juice
1¼ cup cold water
½ tsp. ground
  allspice
1½ tsp. grated
  lemon rind
2 tblsp. honey
3 cloves
1 liter ginger ale
ice

Equipment
2-qt. punch bowl
mixing spoon

1 Mix all the ingredients in the punch bowl and add the ginger ale.

2 Serve with crushed ice.

Glossary

Allspice A spice that is native to the Caribbean. It is sold either as a small red berry or ground into a powder. It is called allspice because its flavor is like a mixture of cinnamon, cloves, and nutmeg.

Ancestors People from whom one is descended, such as grandparents.

Anglican The Church of England or any associated church.

Arawaks The native people of the Caribbean. The Arawaks were a peace-loving people who were forced out of the Greater Antilles by the Caribs.

Caribs A group of native people from South America. They came to the Caribbean and took territory away from the Arawaks, who were living there at that time. The Caribbean and the Caribbean Sea were named for the Caribs.

Cassava A root vegetable shaped like a carrot with brown skin and white flesh.

Christianity A religion based on the teachings of Jesus Christ.

Christians People who follow the teachings of Jesus Christ.

Colony A region that is ruled by another country.

Descendant Someone who comes after a particular person in a family tree.

Diet The sort of food a person generally eats.

Export To sell goods to another country.

Fertile When referring to soil, fertile means the soil is very rich and nourishing, encouraging plant growth.

Gourd A vegetable that belongs to the same family as a pumpkin. Gourds have a hard outer skin and firm flesh and grow on trailing vines.

Hibiscus A type of flowering plant that grows in warm climates. The flowers can be used to flavor drinks.

Hindu Someone who believes in Hinduism, the main religion of India.

Import To buy goods from

another country.

Indentured laborer A person who is hired by a contract to work for a set period of time, usually for very low wages.

Independence When referring to countries, independence means being totally separate and self-governing.

Mace The outer covering of a nutmeg. Mace is bright red when the nutmeg is picked, but it dries to a deep orange. It has a stronger flavor than nutmeg.

Marinated Steeped in a mixture of vinegar, oil, herbs, or other ingredients to add flavor.

Muslims Followers of the religion of Islam and the teachings of the prophet Mohammed.

Nutmeg The hard, brown seed of the nutmeg fruit. The spice known as mace also grows inside the nutmeg fruit, forming a covering around the nutmeg seed.

Pickled To preserve a food in saltwater or vinegar.

Plantation A large area of land used to grow a single crop, such as sugarcane.

Ramadan A month of fasting in the Muslim religion, when people say extra prayers and give money to the poor.

Roman Catholicism A Christian religion. The head of the Roman Catholic Church is the Pope.

Root vegetable A vegetable that grows under the ground.

Roti A type of flat bread made without a rising agent such as yeast. Roti is a typical bread made in India.

Slave A person who is owned as the property of another person.

Standard of living The manner in which people live and the number of goods they can afford to buy.

Tradition A way of doing something that has not changed for years.

Tropics The area of the world around the equator (an imaginary line around the middle of the earth). In the tropics it is hot all year long.

Vegan A person who does not eat meat, fish, or any animal products, including milk, cheese, and eggs.

Vegetarian A person who does not eat meat or fish.

Volcano An opening in the earth's crust through which molten rock, rock fragments, and gases come out from inside the earth, usually with a huge eruption.

Books to read

Hull, Robert. *Caribbean Stories*. Tales from Around the World. New York: Thomson Learning, 1994.

Lerner Geography Staff. *Jamaica in Pictures*. Visual Geography. Minneapolis: Lerner Publications, 1987.

Springer, Eintou Pearl. *The Caribbean*. Revised Edition. Morristown, NJ: Silver Burdett Press, 1987.

Wilkes, Angela. *My First Cookbook*. New York: Alfred A. Knopf, 1989.

Picture acknowledgments

The publishers would like to thank the following for allowing their photographs to be reproduced: Anthony Blake Photo Library 21; Chapel Studios: Zul *cover inset*, 42; Eye Ubiquitous 36 (Trip); Cephas Picture Library 33 bottom (Daniel Czap); J. Allan Cash 6 both, 7 top, 8 top, 11 top, 13 top, 18 top, 19 both, 22; Greg Evans International Picture Library 18 bottom, 20 bottom, 33; Mary Evans Picture Library 9, 10, 12, 13 bottom; GeoScience Film Picture Library 15; Robert Harding Picture Library 8 bottom (K. Gillham); Panos Pictures 20 top (Philip Wolmuth), 23 bottom (Philip Wolmuth), 24 (Philip Wolmuth), 25 top left (Susan I. Cunningham), 40 (Neil Cooper); Planet Earth Pictures 33 top right; Tony Stone Worldwide *title page* (Bob Krist), 4 (Paul Kenward), 7 bottom (Gary Heiss), 11 bottom (Doug Armand), 14 (David Madison), 16 bottom (Peter Poulides), 17 (Richard Bradbury), 29 (Bob Krist), 30 (Dough Armand), 31 (Oliver Benn), 32 (Bob Thomas), 44 (Arthur Tilley); Tropix 23 top left and right (G. Barnish), 27 (Lynn Seldon), 37 (A. & S. Higgins); Wayland Picture Library *cover* (David Cumming), 16 top, 26 (John Wright), 38 (John Wright).

The map artwork on page 5 was supplied by Peter Bull. The recipe artwork on pages 33 to 44 was supplied by Judy Stevens.

Index